Earth in Action

Tsunamis

by Mari Schuh

Consulting Editor: Gail Saunders-Smith, PhD

Consultant: Susan L. Cutter, PhD
Carolina Distinguished Professor and Director,
Hazards & Vulnerability Research Institute
Department of Geography, University of South Carolina

CAPSTONE
press

Mankato, Minnesota

Pebble Plus is published by Capstone Press,
151 Good Counsel Drive, P.O. Box 669, Mankato, Minnesota 56002.
www.capstonepub.com

072011
006231CGVMI

 Books published by Capstone Press are manufactured with paper
containing at least 10 percent post-consumer waste.

Library of Congress Cataloging-in-Publication Data
Schuh, Mari, 1975–
    Tsunamis / by Mari Schuh.
      p. cm. — (Pebble plus. Earth in action)
    Includes bibliographical references and index.
    Summary: "Describes tsunamis, how they occur, and the damage they cause" — Provided by publisher.
    ISBN 978-1-4296-3438-0 (library binding)
    1. Tsunamis — Juvenile literature. I. Title. II. Series.
GC221.5.S45 2010
551.46'37 — dc22   2009002175

Editorial Credits
Erika L. Shores, editor; Lori Bye, designer; Wanda Winch, media researcher

Photo Credits
AP Images/Dita Alangkara, 21; Gemunu Amarasinghe, 5
Capstone Press/Linda Clavel, Patrick Dentinger, 4, 7
Getty Images Inc./AFP/AFP, 15; AFP/Eric Skitzi, 17
iStockphoto/George Clerk, 13
Newscom/AFP/Jhon Bonilla, 9; Getty Images/AFP/Joanne Davis, cover
Shutterstock/Kristian Sekulic, 1; Steven Collins, 19
The Pacific Tsunami Museum/Yasuki Arakaki Collection/Cecilio Licos, 11

The author dedicates this book to her husband's longtime friend Charles Daniel Ruemping.

Note to Parents and Teachers

The Earth in Action set supports national science standards related to earth science.
This book describes and illustrates tsunamis. The images support early readers in understanding
the text. The repetition of words and phrases helps early readers learn new words. This book
also introduces early readers to subject-specific vocabulary words, which are defined in the
Glossary section. Early readers may need assistance to read some words and to use the Table of
Contents, Glossary, Read More, Internet Sites, and Index sections of the book.

Table of Contents

What Is a Tsunami?

A tsunami is a set
of huge ocean waves.
Tsunami is the Japanese word
for harbor wave.

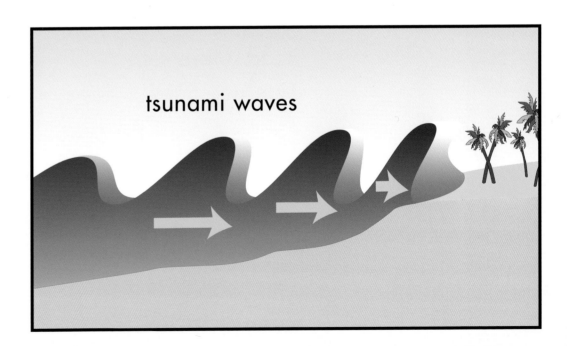

tsunami waves

Tsunamis sometimes happen
when the ocean floor shifts.
Ocean water then moves
up and down and
back and forth.

How Tsunamis Form

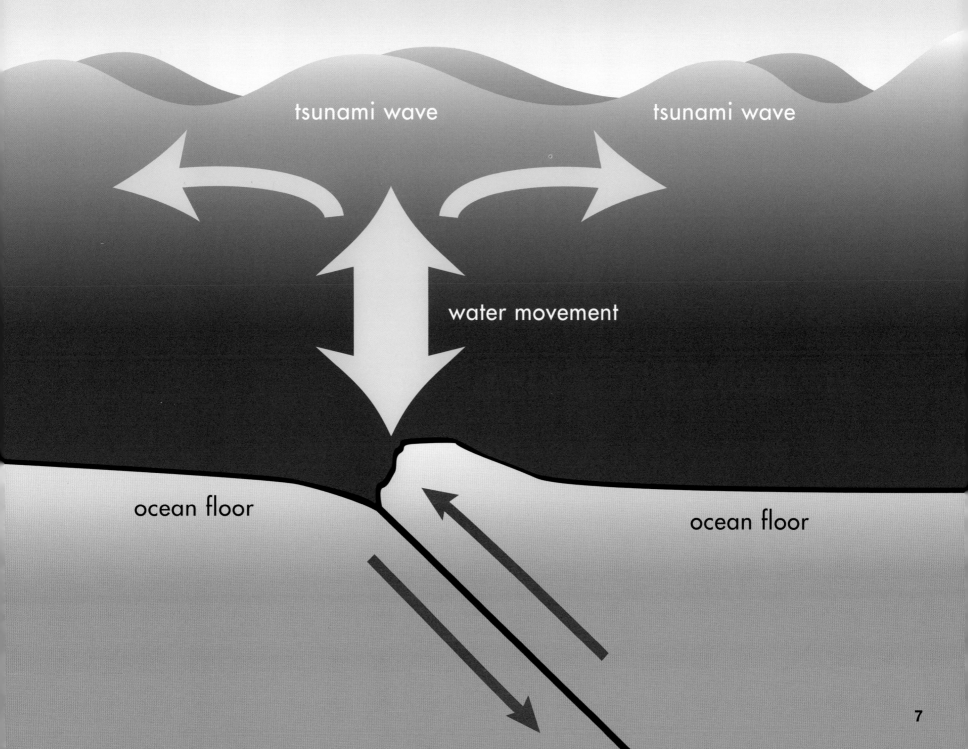

tsunami wave

tsunami wave

water movement

ocean floor

ocean floor

Underwater earthquakes
cause most tsunamis.
Other causes are landslides
and volcanoes. Dirt or lava
hit the water to make waves.

Where Tsunamis Happen

Most tsunamis happen
in the Pacific Ocean.

Tsunamis can travel a long way.

An earthquake in Alaska

can cause a tsunami in Hawaii.

Before a Tsunami

Some places have sirens

to warn a tsunami is coming.

People should move

to higher ground

away from the ocean.

Tsunamis often happen
with little warning.
As a tsunami nears land,
water may be sucked back
from shore.

When a Tsunami Hits

Tsunami waves are

small in the deep ocean.

The waves get bigger

in shallow water near land.

Then the waves crash onto shore.

A wall of water floods

all land near shore.

Cars, houses, and debris

are scattered everywhere.

After a Tsunami

Big tsunamis destroy

almost everything in their paths.

It takes a long time before

life returns to normal.

Glossary

debris — the pieces of something that has been broken

destroy — to break something; tsunamis can destroy houses, buildings, and entire towns.

earthquake — the sudden shaking of the earth's surface

harbor — a place where ships load and unload their supplies

landslide — a large mass of earth and rocks that suddenly slides down a mountain or hill

shallow — not deep

shore — the place where the ocean meets land

volcano — an opening in the earth's surface that sometimes sends out hot lava, steam, and ash

Read More

Armentrout, David, and Patricia Armentrout. *Tsunamis.* Earth's Power. Vero Beach, Fla.: Rourke, 2007.

Bullard, Lisa. *Tsunamis.* Pull Ahead Books. Forces of Nature. Minneapolis: Lerner, 2009.

Wendorff, Anne. *Tsunamis.* Blastoff! Readers. Extreme Weather. Minneapolis: Bellwether Media, 2009.

Internet Sites

FactHound offers a safe, fun way to find Internet sites related to this book. All of the sites on FactHound have been researched by our staff.

Here's all you do:

Visit *www.facthound.com*

FactHound will fetch the best sites for you!

Index

Word Count: 174

Grade: 1

Early-Intervention Level: 24